John Hughes was born in Belfast in 1962. Educated at Queen's University, Belfast and the University of Ulster, he has published three collections of poetry: *The Something In Particular* (Gallery Press, 1986), *Negotiations with the Chill Wind* (Gallery Press, 1991) and *The Devil Himself* (Gallery Press, 1996). He lives in Co. Donegal with his family.

By the same author

FAST FORWARD

FAST FORWARD

JOHN HUGHES

LAGAN PRESS
BELFAST
2003

Acknowledgements
The author would like to acknowledge the editors of the following magazines in which some of these poems first appeared: *Poetry Ireland Review*, *Thumbscrew* and *Poetry London*.

Published by
Lagan Press
138 University Avenue
Belfast BT7 1GZ

ARTS
COUNCIL
of Northern Ireland

ISBN: 1 873687 79 6
Author: Hughes, John
Title: Fast Forward
2003

Set in Sabon
Cover: Psycho Pomp (1986) by Martin Wedge
(*reproduced courtesy of the artist
and the Arts Council of Northern Ireland*)
Design: December Publications
Printed by Easyprint, Belfast

for Eoin and Cartha

Contents

The Dark Oaks Stayed Strangely Still

I knew how much fear was in my father
When he took me aside after the rosary

And said, 'That I was the terror of that woman
Was the most natural thing in the world.'

Like the coward I was I said nothing,
And set off to burn the soiled bedlinen

Beyond the dark oaks that hold the house in shadow,
Be there winter sun or summer rain.

Such an absurd day. A dog lay at the foot of the bed,
Listening to the corpse's putrefying innards groan and growl.

Snow swirled in from the moon-blanched glen.
Neighbours made their way through the dark oaks

To the bedside of one dressed in the blue garments of Mary,
Of one who'd cried and screamed and prayed—

As if that could stop the uncontrollable shitting,
Drooling and puking.

And I wondered how long I would have to stay
In the country of winter's dregs, of spectral grey.

All around the house the Donegal wind twisted and turned,
And yet, and yet, the dark oaks stayed strangely still.

Consummation

So, there was Tony waving the umbrella over his tonsured head
As the Bastille Day fireworks illuminated hundreds of stone roses
All around us Algerians took one another by the hand
And marvelled at the red, the white and the blue.

Tony dived into the filthy stillness of the Seine
And swam upstream to dally with the Mohammedans,
Until their dread of him disappeared
With the rising of the watery sun.

When Tony turned the key in his door
He knew he'd lost me. He knew he'd never had me.
He thought of naming names, revealing dates and times,
Of making the same mistake twice.

I'd drawn Jupiter, Venus and Saturn
On every wall of his tiny apartment.
That made him mad as hell. What did Tony do?
He wrote a sonnet. And another. And another.

Sonnets about a pond edged with greyish leaves,
Drinking coffee over pie, goods trains coming and going,
Total dark, Jamaica Street in July, broken crockery,
Boats tugging against their ropes, tumours on the brain.

Only when he shyly looked into my unblinking eyes
Could I let him sleep in a bed
That smelt, I swear, of burning flesh.
Tony wouldn't have had it any other way.

Questions, Questions

And when you closed the door of deepest green behind you,
Who or what did you come upon?

Was it a man who soiled himself with excitement
As he smashed every stick of furniture in the house?

Or was it a teenage girl who undressed you
With a knife and fork?

Or was it a dog, with red eyes and rotten teeth,
That lay down at your feet

And waited for you to put a knitting needle
Through the right atrium of its all-too-human heart?

Don't Ask

Mullaghdrin is where you chose to meet with
The seventh son of the only son of a seventh son,

Who taught you how to chop down an ash tree
With nothing more than the nib of a fountain pen,

Who taught you how to heal a greenstick fracture
With lemon balm and a carpenter's gouge.

And what did the pair of you talk about?
You say nothing. He says everything.

Judge, Jury, Executioner

Before judgement is passed upon him,
The man looks up at me with the eyes of a bird.
There is no wind. He cries for his mother.

When he is reborn, it'll be as a man
Who'll look up at me with the eyes of a bird.
There'll be no wind. He'll cry for his mother.

He is face to face with me:
I don't know anything about God.

Shroud

All alone this ten years. The oaks and elms are gone a month.
Each dawn since, he regrets cutting them down.

With the trees-piles of firewood stacked behind the byre,
He understands why they were planted the year he was born,

For the house looks out upon a lake the colour of gunmetal,
That in the windless gloom seems to stretch a hundred miles.

Colder than the icy lake-water he wraps himself in a blanket
And prepares himself to be charming.

I tell him that his daughter will not come,
Not until he will sign over with good grace

The ten acres of rushes and whins that is her due.
After a silence that might have lasted a year

He asks me, 'Does the wee bitch ever speak of me kindly?
I used to be her daddy. Hard to believe, eh?'

He coughs yellowy-green phlegm into the palm of his hand
And then smirks slyly at my pretending not to notice.

So much for him; he's only weeks away
From lending his body to death.

As he wonders at how 72 years have come to this,
I suddenly remember the distance I must travel.

As my car scrunches its way out of the scurfy yard,
He returns to washing his bloody sheet, his spotless shroud.

The Brains of the Operation

In the course of hunting feral cats and wounded foxes,
Driving tanker-loads of diesel and van-loads of *Embassy Regal*,
I cross the border a hundred times a day.

At Lifford, I rest beneath the oaks till noon,
At Killea, I pull rushes from under the feet of old men,
On Clady bridge I swallow the pebbles that line my pockets.

Ever since I witnessed my barber being shot in the head
By a retard whose hair he'd cut since the age of seven,
I have believed 32 is a magical number.

I can wake in a ditch with a thousand pounds in my pocket
And know nothing of how they came to be there.
I'm a rare creature for I can smell blood from a mile off.

Often I'm dragged into the back of a Land Rover or Ford Granada
To have my privates twisted and pulled
By slack-jawed peelers who think it a kind of party game.

For a week now I've made camp on the shores of Mullaghmore,
Where I make note of stars that have not been seen
Since the night before Lord Mountbatten went the way of all flesh.

I'm a man who can swallow his own hand,
Who has never told a joke against himself,
Who knows the etymology of *saveloy*.

At the Death

I

Because my right arm is dead,
I know the worst is not over yet.

I wake in the ultrawhite light
To hear Miss Sumner cutting winter-wood.

II

Her eyes sting as she remembers
Holy Cross burning through the night.

She spits on her callused hands
And wonders if she is truly a bigot.

III

This morning threatens rain and tearing winds.
My feet are cold and I want to sing.

In the darkness, my father waits for me.
His face is crueller than I ever remember.

IV

When a robin beats against the bedroom window
My father is like a man called to order.

At the death he will feel important and wise,
But as ever, nothing he says will make any sense.

And Look What That Led To

When you laughed at her proposal
Of a life in, of all places, Portstewart,
You knew, you just knew, a can of petrol
Would be poured the full length of the hall—
That you'd get down on your hands and knees
To thank Christ you weren't at home, amidst the half-eaten
Pizza, crushed beer cans, broken crockery, author's copies,
Listening to the north wind roaring down the chimney,
As the lit match was pushed through the letter box.

The Battle of Ballynahinch

Fearing fear itself, General Munro's cat says,
Whet up yer knife boys and whistle up yer dogs,
For I am past caring, I am past all.

She devours me as if I were ice and snow.
Later, her blue claws as sharp as my scimitar,
She'll eat what is left of the left-for-dead.

The Coming of the Dead in Winter

Sitting on a bough of the fallen yew,
Panic seizes me. I cry out to stars
That have been dead a thousand years,
The names of all for whom you are tears.

I am compelled to cut open my stomach
And examine the weight and shape
Of the frozen blossoms I devoured so greedily
When we lived on the edge of fields

That smelt of rain, nothing else;
And in which nothing grew but the noiseless wind
That is colder than your dishevelled corpse
On this, the day after Resurrection Day.

Saving the Union

Cold north wind. Everlasting day almost upon us.
Across Glengall Street, dogs scatter in packs of five and six,
As a black dog devours your discarded shadow.

Just as your black tongue touches my black tongue,
I desire that you tell me if you spat three times
On the mound of clay you moulded me from.

Strange, your breath smells of neither one of us.
And who is it you wait here so patiently for? Is he one of us?
Tell me so that I can have my death fit and rattle.

Fast Forward

The camcorder records it as being midnight.
On the table in front of me: a bar of *Turkish Delight*,
A platter of roast beef, a sprig of parsley,
Dubie's *Alehouse Sonnets*, Blur's *Country Life*,
A zinker bullet and a photograph of Marco Van Basten.

I lift my eyes from the long oak table
To stare at the two moons over Gortalaia.
As I make my unsteady way to the VCR,
Faint with tiredness and three bottles of poor chianti,
The day's images take a hold of me:

Squat Boyle kicking lumps out of his lame dog,
A high voltage generator surrounded by whitethorn,
A mutilated seal thrown into the back of a Transit van,
The rainburst that took us by surprise
As we grunted and growled from our very depths.

So drunk am I that I don't see the pine bough
You've laid across my stripped bed,
The carving knife placed upon my fat pillow.
In the darkness I listen to my lungs fill with fluid.
And then years go by, as they do. It is a minute to midnight.

Having Sold My Soul to the Devil

The ferryman had crossed translucent Loughros More
Bearing gifts of *Embassy Regal* and *Smirnoff Blue*.
Rebecca wouldn't let me flatten him when he whined,
'Why does the sight of him make me sick?'
Instead, I pulled a blue and white chair up to the door
And listened to the wind hurt the world.

As luciferous rain came down off the mountains,
The ferryman bowed his head and vomited.
Rebecca cleaned up the mess with the back of her hand,
And a sheet of paper on which was scrawle:,
I love you more than ever. Six oranges and Domestos.
Hugs and kisses. Ajax, Bisto, Daz. Screw you.

I can't tell you how much it unsettled me when they kissed.
I stepped outside into the lovely, chilly gloaming
To stare at the January sky. She bolted the door behind me.
The stars unnerved me. The moon terrified me.
And then I remembered the ferryman's name
Was the same as my own.

I hammered on the door like a Force 10 gale.
An hour I waited and still she would not let me in.
I threw stones through every window. I shat on her doorstep.
I collapsed under the great oak that overhung our house:
The tree I planted to mark her marriage
To the devil to whom I'd given my name.

Cold Ashes

Why should she not leave it too late
To take my cold hand in her cold hand,
And talk of the bleakness of these parts
When the wind comes from Donegal;

Of the blood and wine and cold ashes
We smeared over one another
The last night we came to know each other
Better than either of us thought wise?

Because I don't know what love is for,
I put my ear to the wall of this hospice room.
What do I hear? A spider spinning a web
To ensnare a single drop of dew.

Because it is time for her to leave me,
I tell her I can hear nothing.
As the moonlight finally reaches our high bed,
I fold up her shadow and am bereft.

Celestial Mechanics

On Ascension Thursday,
I change the oil in my VW Passat.
Walking back to the house to scrub my hands,
I think of my friend, dead of cancer a week:
Forever from of old, men have been so;
And none born can escape this thing.

Christ Almighty. I turn on my heels:
I've forgotten to replace the fanbelt.

Last Winter

The bowl of green apples is devoured
By a woman who has a spot on her lung.

Why is she filled with horror
At the ardent glances of a man half her age?

She washes the bowl and smashes it
Against the varicose wall.

Meanwhile, the wind does its worst
With the frail moon, the fading stars.

Nothing But Nothing

Quaffing a flagon of cider in the dark woods,
I attempt to hide my sweaty, unwaning ardour
From Kathleen McCabe of Newbliss,
As she explains how much cleverer she is than me:

For Kathleen McCabe can count to thirty,
Speaks German with a Monaghan accent,
Has shoplifted in Clones, Cavan and Cologne.
And understands that I am not to be trusted.

Night after night there's the same performance:
Kathleen McCabe stands with her back to mine
And recites the names of the men she's slept with
For the price of a burger or a bottle of *Smirnoff Ice*.

When I put my hands around her throat,
Kathleen McCabe pushes me away and suggests a journey,
Along the grey, stony path which circles the lough,
To the domain of the robin and the wren.

But not one foot is set in front of the other,
For we are finally brought to our knees by the cider.
She promises she'll surrender to the sky and the night,
Whatever she means by that.

Come morning we wake with our entrails spilling out,
Our limbs chopped off and buried in ten different places.
In the dark woods nothing is impossible.
Nothing but nothing.

Promises and Warnings

Abandoned at birth on a dark and stormy Sabbath—
Out of fear and wrath and disgust—

I've grown up to the shadow
Of the holy mountain of Muckish.

Though I am darkness I am light.
Though I am not light I am not darkness.

When I tire of such metaphysics,
I'll cover myself with sharp stones and dead leaves

And listen to the promises and warnings
Of the trees in the westerlies,

Until I rise from my grave
In the moist depths of a burning forest.

Beyond death, I'll flit across Muckish
Under a sky as dark and stormy as Heaven.

The Rest of Our Lives

The Chinook swooped in low from the east.
I remember wondering how long I had bored you.

We played the game of counting out in Irish
The number of paras scattering across the rushy fields.

As the helicopter wheeled back round towards Bessbrook,
You said your mind was made up once and for all.

As the last para disappeared behind a line of whins,
The wind and rain, which has not stopped since, began to fall.

And worse again, the walk back to the car
Took us through the churning forest of Douglas Firs,

In which are said to lie the graves of two informers—
Their lips sewn fast with stitches of linen thread.

I was a hostage to myself if I did not ask,
Do you really think I am a parasite? A waster? A creep?

Before you could answer we were surrounded by soldiers
Going about HMG's covert business.

Where are you going? Where are you coming from?
Why shouldn't we just shoot you where you stand?

And so began the rest of our lives.

Heaven on Earth

A silver Mercedes Benz convertible roars east,
And out of its dust cloud appears Christ the Redeemer.
We down our third beer in as many minutes:
We know better than to offer Him one,
For He'll not drink with the likes of us.

I rub my left hand in the ochre dust
And make the sign of the cross
On his acne-pitted forehead.
He spits in my face and wanders off
In the general direction of the railyard.

By evening, we'll have reached our destination—
A one-room Quonset hut overlooking a Texaco refinery,
A *Burger King* and a Firestone factory.
We'll make it our home from home
By lighting fires in each corner of the room,

Pissing in the sink, smearing our shit over the walls
And ourselves from scalp to toe.
We'll lie in the middle of the floor mumbling *The Lord's Prayer*,
Pretending we're not who we say we are.
It must be so. It must, must, must.

The Sentence is Death

My hangover is so bad (depression and sickness in equal measure
That I seek some solace in my old diaries.
Well, well. Apparently in 1981 I thought of nothing else
But of walking among Tollymore's sweet pine,
My cold hand in the cold hand of Ellie Patterson.

If memory serves me, that summer was mostly spent in my room
Listening to the Pye radio crackle and hiss
With news from the next parish to our own:
Of Yellow Malones and White O'Hares dragged from their beds
And shot in the back of their Fenian heads.

And then there was 1983. The year I woke alone,
Night after night, in a house that had lost half its roof to the wir
I'd stare up at the moon and the stars of a strange parish,
Where nothing in the way of murder and mutilation
Was enough to make me want to leave.

And now? I spend my time watching what I say
To the shock-headed toe-rags who are Death & Co.
A long time ago, I thought the world a secret to be discovered.
I was a different person then: I was enthralled with myself.
I was true to myself. I could make you die.

Tout

All summer I dreamt of the scraggy fields,
In which were buried the battered remains

Of those who spoke too freely and too often
About neighbours out and about at some ungodly hour.

All week Manhattan had withstood electric storms out
    of *King Lear*.
Dumbstruck by each other we lay in their dazzling dark.

All summer I'd drink too much *Paddy* and walk
    into the furniture,
Shouting the odds about serious steps lightly taken,

Of the hacked-off fingers and thumbs of this informer,
The burns and scalds of that informer.

Towards summer's end Susan had enough.
She hit me across the face with a *Le Creuset* saucepan

And told me you didn't need to be dead to be dead.
I had been found out at last and I was never happier.

I shook my head wearily in a way that was meant to say,
Try teaching me the arts of rage. Go on.

Remembrance Day

Three-legged chairs, clapped-out fridges, dead dogs,
William Scott's brushes, *Kosangas* cylinders,
    an abandoned Dormobile.
I'm walking through a dump in County Fermanagh.

I've been walking since my horse threw me last night.
If only I had the hands of a Taafe or a McCoy,
I'd be at home watching the stars that are neither
    right nor wrong.

Today I'll meet a horseman with bloodshot eyes and bad teeth.
He'll tell his nag to remind me hell is constant and eternal,
That I'll be dead or dying in 22 hours.

We'll sit by the rushy side of the road to Ederney,
Smoking a couple of packs of *Embassy Regal*,
Watching the Vauxhalls and Volkswagens roar by.

I've dreamed this dream so often it makes less and less sense...
In the town of Enniskillen, the west wind rises up and tosses me
Over a double chain-link fence embroidered with red poppies.

Lying among the dead, the armless, legless and eyeless,
Among the groaning and shrieking, the whimpering and sobbing,
I understand that I am no less a stranger to them
    than I am to myself.

Confession

Father, it maddens me that I must tolerate
A man whose religion of cherubim and seraphim
Has made him skilful in all forms of ignorance.

In the foyer of the Europa Hotel,
He's scratching and fondling a little black dress
Who earns a crust studying the brains of stillbirths.

This one can make fires that give off no heat.
He even knows why she's in thrall to one
Who sooner or later will beat her within an inch of her life.

Come eleven, when he takes a black taxi home,
I'll warn him about the morose grunters and the grinning howlers
Who keep coming back for less and less.

What will become of him? A story you'll have heard too often:
He'll bleed too much for one with the likes of me to keep,
And I'll throw him to the dogs on the street.

All Belfast will stop to have a look,
And not one will lift a finger
To save the dogs from his cold flesh.

I Do Not Like Thee

On those rare nights when the mist lifts
And the sky brims with stars,
You can hear them sing songs
Of bony girls in communion dresses,
With bullet holes where their eyes should be.
You love it when she bites your tongue
And twists your cock so hard
That your screams drown them out.

Is it they who come calling once a century,
Their attack dogs trotting nine paces behind,
To ask you to confirm they are long dead
And yammer prayers to their gods of mist and stars?
Is it true what they say? That you always say no?
That they never set the dogs on your soul?

Pillow Talk

I wake out of a dream of biting into your flesh
To discover it tastes like rotten apples,

And raise myself up on one arm to vow yet again
Never ever to drink *Liebfraumilch* by a full moon.

You lie across my chest and ask me question after question:
Who are you? Which one of us smells so bad?

Was it you who threw up in the bath and kitchen sink?
Were you the fucker who wrecked my hi-fi?

As the questions keep coming,
Last night comes back to me little by little:

West of the Bann is ours to have and to hold.
Six pints of Harp and half a bottle of Paddy.

Paddy Reilly murdering 'The Fields of Athenry',
Puking my guts into an avocado bath.

The TV turned up as Big Gerry waves regally
From an armour-plated black taxi.

A DUP poster tossed onto the fire.
Five pints of Smithwicks and half a bottle of Black Bush.

A pair of Trillick shinners saying I wasn't right in the head
When I tried to explain that to remember you must forget.

A strapless dress, bra, and tights.
A tangle of arms and legs.

As for your questions, what can I tell you
That you don't already know?

That'll stop you asking again and again
What exactly it was we should never ever have done.

The Abercorn

The tea leaves in my cup tell of flies swarming a bloated belly.
At the next table sits a man in a sharp suit
Who asks the beautiful waitress if it is true
She is the mother-to-be of a bastard.
She crouches like a beggar and brushes up the crumbs
That have fallen at his size 10 foot.
The waitress is missing an arm, the sharp suit a leg.
Only I know they are immortal.

Don't you care for me? he says bitterly.
The waitress slaps him hard across the face.
The sharp suit kicks her in the shins.
Whereupon she punches him in the right eye.
My mother asks for the bill.
The waitress smiles sweetly at me.
Outside there are screeches and bellowings.
I know what awaits me out there.
I'm 9 years of age and I want to die.

The Wardrobe

Twenty-five years have passed since last I laid eyes
On this battered wardrobe—the Saturday evening
My father hauled it downstairs to barricade the front door.

While his wife and children tossed and turned in their beds,
My father nailed lengths of sweet-smelling 4x2
Across every window on the ground floor.

Come morning, his face as white as the refrigerator,
He laid a hurley stick on the kitchen table and told me:
Hobgoblin, nor foul fiend, should daunt our spirit.

For hours on end, I watched snow fall on the Oldpark,
Covering Sam McCrum's Hillman Hunter,
The brains of Mrs. Zukor's knocked-down Pomeranian.

Bored with fear, I changed into my mothballed Sunday best,
And in a room dark and quiet as my brain
I waited for our killers to make their way from Silverstream.

On Monday morning the removal men arrived.
I remember so clearly how they dropped the wardrobe
As they lumbered along the icy garden path,

How eagerly I tore the perfect wings from the moths
That came fluttering,
Fluttering out of its stinking darkness.

Royal Portrush

Through all of July and the first days of August,
Mutilated cats were found hanging from lamp posts,

On the steps of the Orange Hall, in Ormo bread vans,
Behind the public toilets where the winos fuck and shit,

In every part of Barry's Amusements,
And strewn across the luxuriant greens of Royal Portrush.

If you'd met the killer, he'd have fucked you
And made you dig your own grave.

Without Name

He pulled his maculated hand out of my mouth
   with such force
It seemed my tongue was on fire.

He gained my trust by revealing to his only son
The smallness of the full-starred heavens of winter.

He smashed the mirror I held up to him,
And devoured his own reflection.

He spat in the face of his only son
For speaking in salamandrine tongues.

* * *

I raised my unblemished hand to one
Who is the tyrant and torturer my faith demands.

I pissed and shit over one
Who always accepts the unacceptable.

I drank the blood and ate the flesh of one
Who drinks my blood and eats my flesh.

I cowered at the bloody feet of one
Whose only sustenance is my sole fear.

Tomorrow is Another Day

From the room at the top of the narrow stairs
Come the wails and moans of your sudden loss.

And then she is gone from the world
Of twenty hundred strange lights in the northern sky,

And winds that blow from Glengesh
As if there were no tomorrow.

Dangerous Driving

The world is hard frost and gritty stars
In the pitch-dark hour before dawn.

It has been a long drive from Rosslare:
I haven't slept since leaving Carentan O Carentan.

At the back of Errigal, I fall asleep and lose control of the car.
There comes a rumble and the moon rushes eastward.

I turn up *Dark Side of the Moon*, and recline the seat
To muse upon the dream I had the previous night—

Of cutting open my brain to discover
It is as odourless as my own shit.

A dream which, according to the Floyd boys,
Signifies I have a fear of dying from bowel cancer.

I clamber out of the car to listen to the wind that is born
Fully formed in the black waters of Iceland.

As a line of fretful sheep appears in the darkness,
I lose my balance and fall sideways into a sheugh.

I lie trembling in the frozen clabber,
My right leg broken in two places.

As the sky grows lighter, I listen to the Icelandic wind
Gather strength for a surge to Connaught,

And think of Eleanor, who had me convinced
I could love her more than myself;

Of Eleanor, who had me convinced
We could live happily high in the Sperrins,

In a cottage with a garden where nothing grew
But nettles and docks, thistles and creeping buttercup,

In whose shady nooks we could close our eyes and smile
Because we no longer spoke in tongues of Benzedrine.

I close my bleary eyes and summon her to my aching side.
She smells of the grave. She is afraid of me.

I wake to find a robin perched on my right leg.
I must break its delicate neck.

What Makes Its Way In Darkness
Ends in Darkness

It was early dark, in the thick of teeming snowfall,
When we veered off the concession road
To meet a stranger with a familiar face.
I don't deserve this were the only words he spoke
As the hood was put over his close-shaven head.

Would that he'd stayed where he belonged—
In the house built by the gallows tree,
Of the rebels of such and such a year,
And the rebels of such and such a year.
Would that our screams had not become his and his alone.

Decisions, Decisions

As Lord Makko was about to raise the deer,
The mastiff lifted its nose out of a book and attacked.
Before Lord Makko could remember its name
The beast had sunk its teeth into his broken left leg.
My lovely Jellen Grame he moaned.
The mastiff lay down at his master's feet and died.

In Liscooley, Altnacarron and Carrickmannon,
They say Lord Makko returned home a different man—
That he licked me with flames instead of his tongue,
That instead of dreaming of the dark woods of Glenaver
He lay awake at night breathing into my mouth,
That he decided to live forever.

My Red Hand In Your Red Hand

I saunter into Dunmore Park, eating a pound of raw mince,
To throw a monkey on a dog called *Distillery Prince*.
It runs in last. Be assured I'll make it my business
To have the cur tortured with pliers and broken glass.

I stomp into The Berlin Arms with the joyous news
That Tommy Herron's corpse lies in Drumbo or thereabouts.
In between choruses of 'The Billy Boys'
I eat my own shite washed down with bottles of *Red Heart*.

I put my shoulder to the door of my little palace
And climb over sheets of corrugated iron,
Rolls of chicken wire, car tyres, breeze blocks,
Spades, pickaxes, and knives of Sheffield steel.

In no time at all, I find myself in the glory hole.
It's clear we'll make a fine pair of butchers—
A boning knife in one red hand,
And a boning knife in the other red hand.

This evening will be like many another of late:
A crate of *Monk Export*, a bag of chips,
And a prayer of thanksgiving as we sit in a black taxi
Making mincemeat of a Fenian's throat, nose, and cock.

Homeless

At four o'clock in the morning, I phoned my wife to tell her
I'd made my last blind man see a green table lamp,
A red biro, a blue snooker ball.

My wife didn't answer.
She lay on the bed pretending she was a pig
With a boning knife stuck in its right flank.

And she lay there she thought of the 100 things
A faith healer's wife must do before she can get out of bed
To watch a TV programme about the Colossus of Rhodes.

Since then I've gone about my business
With no village or house in sight.
I live rough. I live off the land. I live to die.

Come night, I light a fire in each corner of a field
That is an illegal dump for chicken carcasses,
And wait to go out of this life of love and benevolence.

Conquest

The rusting Cortina can't be seen from the road:
Abandoned in this plantation acre by your eldest brother,
A few days before he emigrated to Canada.

We lie down beside it and eat bread and cheese,
Drink a warm bottle of cider, and smoke a pack of *Rothmans*.
It's your 19th birthday and I present you with a Claddagh ring.

Just as we're about to put our clothes back on,
There's an explosion. You're 100 per cent sure it's a landmine.
Suddenly, I feel heavy in my body. You burst out laughing.

No more than a mile away, runs the road to Draperstown.
As a plume of black-grey smoke rises above it,
We fall back into the long grass and blue cornflowers.

You stroke my cheek and say we should be on our way,
That as long as you've my blood on your hands
I'll never see you again.

Birthday Boy
for Jerome Crolly

I remember how I stood cold and far from my magic books,
In the company of a pig fattened for slaughter:
Waiting for Dawson Priestly to take off his police uniform,
Put on his killing clothes and take a knife to the pig's throat.

I'd been six as long as I could remember,
And since winter had promised myself the pig's tongue.
But that was not to be. The pig tore free of its tether
And disappeared into the bowels of the earth.

There was nothing for it but to kick off my *Tuf* shoes,
And go inside to have my cake and eat it.
For the longest time I stared at the seven candy-stripe candles
And listened to the hierarchic voice of the BBC

Describe the scented dark of the Bogside:
CS gas, a county inspector's dog-breath, salt rain,
Chicken guts, *Monk Export*, sour milk,
Dirty linen, coal smoke, and 22lbs of rotting dog.

No matter about the coming of night,
The dark police everywhere and nowhere,
The seventh candle could not be blown out,
No matter how much I huffed and puffed—

To blow the house down around a boy
Who'd sworn he'd dip his fingers in hot pig blood.
How wondrous and mighty strange these events seem now
To one who lies in his bed, reeking of vomit and booze
    and rotting teeth.

The Peep o' Day

What passed between us was a dare.
At the peep o' day, you swam Lough Bradan
With a bag of stones strapped to your broad back.

By the time you'd reached the other shore,
I was halfway home to my red-haired wife
Who sits all day in a darkened room

Rubbing the buboes in her armpits with salt and vinegar,
Laughing and jeering at a boy
Who is said to be her flesh and blood.

By the time you reached the tree-lined path to our house,
The boy was being beaten from room to room
By one who believes him not to be his mother's son.

You came upon me, Captain Rock,
Dressed in a white shirt, my wife's blue gingham dress,
And a straw hat festooned with white ribbons.

Captain, Captain, do you remember what you said?
That I had betrayed you at the peep o' day,
That a ghost-faced soldier was waiting on the other shore?

You barred the doors and drank the health
Of those who'd died at Derry, Aughrim and the Boyne.
Only then did I speak. Except I didn't.

Often Enough

Too often, it seems that my work is not appreciated. Too often my toys are tied to stakes and burnt as the possessed playthings of witches. As the flames reach high into the November sky, I eat marmalade sandwiches and plan how I will get home alive.

Often, I join my toys at the stake.

Often, my executioners eat my marmalade sandwiches.

Toy-maker, they say your mother makes sandwiches that taste of shit. We love them. We do, we do, we do.

Leopold of the Belgians

At the fancy-dress party, my fellow toy-makers jig about and talk dirty to the local doctors' wives. As I've done every year since the illegal partition of our emerald isle, I've come as Leopold of the Belgians. Every year, since 1954, I spend the evening sitting between Roger Casement and Mark Twain. Every 16 minutes a waiter brings me a pint of Guinness and a ball of malt. The waiter tells me he has reared a crossbreed—a half-dog, half-sheep. How Borgesian I remark. He smirks and tells me his name is Russell Edson.

And then it begins, as it does every year. My fellow toy-makers sit down beside me to tell me how, for the rest of their lives, they'll make nothing but toys that come to life—toys that'll snuggle up to little children, and tell them tales of princes who're skewered on their own swords by the fair princesses they've come to rescue. It's a sickness this desire of theirs to keep me sitting here, grinning from ear to ear until the lights come on and our national anthem is played too fast, much too fast. The only escape is to fall asleep, and dream I'm not dreaming I'm Leopold of the Belgians eating monkey brains and, of course, Brussels sprouts.

The Toy-Maker's Wife Sleeps In

At a minute past nine, I burst through the swing-doors of the Tyrconnell Toyshop. Before security can stop me I pull from the shelves a *Hitari tumbler*, a *Scalextric Jaguar* and a *Smoby* quad.

I pull off my *Caterpillar* boots and jump up and down on them until my feet bleed.

When security catch up with me (at a minute past ten) they phone my wife to tell her my gut is full of worms, my breath smells of rotten meat, the collar of my mauve *Charvet* shirt is spotless; that when they open up my head they found nothing but sawdust, that when ...

My wife hangs up on them, and turns her attention back to tying a highwayman's hitch around her neck, stubbing out cigarettes on the back of her hand, painting her lips with dog-shit, and the hundred other things a toy-maker's wife must do before she can get out of bed in the morning.

Amnesia

In my cupboards you will find the tools of my former trade. These consist of a quill pen, two nails, an Indian club, a pair of pinking shears, a pound of mince steak, a mouse's heart, coffee dregs, two shopping bags of raw sienna, an onion hoe, the mandible of a grey seal, and a 9mm parabellum round.

What was my trade? If I knew that I would not scream foul abuse at little children on their way to school, throw bricks at horses in fields, kick small black dogs from one end of the street to the other, or worst of all write poems about bright green signs in the night, cigarette boxes, seawalls of concrete and steel, sick headaches, ankle-length shorts, electric fans, ambulances, launderettes, cantilever bridges, deckchairs, blood-soaked wrens, Jesus Christ himself digging my grave.